THE
PSYCHIC
NEXT
DOOR

THE PSYCHIC NEXT DOOR

DEBORAH BATTY COLYER

WHATS NEXT VISIONS, LLC

Printed in the United States of America

WHATS NEXT VISIONS, LLC

Broomall, PA

WhatsNextVisions@gmail.com

First Edition, December, 2017

ISBN 10:   0692996923

ISBN 13:   978-0692996928

DEDICATION

This book is dedicated to my wonderful parents for giving me an idyllic and magical childhood. They made our ordinary lives extraordinary. Also to Gary Sr., Gary Jr., and Nicholas for completing the circle.

To my sister Shirley: we've lived our lives side by side, sharing the ups and downs, the laughter and the tears. No matter what life may bring, I am so happy to be traveling this path with you as my sister.

ACKNOWLEDGEMENTS

I have been so fortunate in this life to have had such a wonderful family, including my parents and my sister Shirley. While Shirley is my beloved blood sister whom I treasure, I have been blessed with chosen sisters as well.

One of these cherished chosen sisters is my dear friend Laurel Jacobs McVaugh, without her help and encouragement this book would never come to fruition. We have been friends and chosen sisters since we met in Collingdale in 1969 when her family moved into the house across the street from ours. Forty-eight years later we are still as close as ever and have strengthened our bond through the creation of this book. I thank the Universe for our kindred souls.

So many people have helped me throughout my career, that to name them all would be to write another book, but I sincerely thank you all.

I would like to give special acknowledgement and express my gratitude to the following family, friends, and businesses whom have played a huge role in supporting and encouraging me throughout my career.

To:

Doug Bright

Tori Bright

Ryan and Erin Bright

Jessica Colyer

Katalin Malcolm, PhD

I am grateful and blessed for all the joy and happiness you have brought to my life.

To:

Clara Florence Scarinci (Auntie)

The Baionno Family

The Batty Family

The Bernatowicz

The Colyer Family

The Detore Family

The Gumbrell Family

The Haughton Family

The Malone Family

Mike Murphy

The Messatzzia Family

The Naylor Family

The Nye Family

The Pearling Family

The Smith Family

The Woods Family

I feel privileged and thankful that we have had the opportunity to travel through this lifetime together.

Thank you to my cherished friends for your encouragement, and abiding support:

Jane and Roger Albany

Jolan Altman

Ariana Barbato

Marge Borek

Judy Brennan

Ray and Eileen Bryant

Dan and Katie Capella

Caroline Catona, DVM

The Causerano/Figorski Family

Marilee Ciarmella

Susan Clark

Terry Coyler

Joann Curry

The Daniels Family

The Ditizio Family

The Duncan Famliy

Hank Eberle

Debbie Fasciocco

Terry Galante

Meredith Gerhard

Lisa Gorson

Lynne Grim

Jaime Harasym

Brenda and Bud Harris

Tom Jerome

Kate Kerr

The Kirman Family

Barb Liberati

Dottie Lieb

Susan Litwin Verticelli

Michael Loro

Michael Madden

Charlie Maurone

Janice McGuigon

Linda McGuigon Stam

Kathy McVeigh

Dan Mills	Gale Simon
Margaret Mills Kelly	Betty Signor
Rich Morella	Sally Smith
The Obie Family	The Steeley Family
Steve Owen	Maria Sykorova Pritz
Marina Parent	Paul Trapuzza
Menakshi Rajan	Jackie and Mark Wheat
Scottie The Psychic	Dave White

A very special thank you to Kim Hill, for her kindness and generosity in sharing her son Rocco's story.

The following businesses have been vital and instrumental both personally and professionally. They have my deepest gratitude, loyalty, and appreciation:

Ackerman Chiropractic Services Inc

Michael A. Burns Esq.

Dr. Kevin Cross, Cross Medical Group

Dr. Stephen E Cross

The Gas Light Restaurant

Rago Griesser & Co

David Jaffe, MD

Rich Leyman, PA, Suburban Pulmonary Medicine

Daniel Martin, MD

The Painted Teacup

Pappano and Breslin, Attorneys at Law

Ridley Adult School

Safari Parties

Taylor Hospice (Residence)

CONTENTS

PART TWO

MOST MEMORABLE PSYCHIC EXPERIENCES

AUTHOR'S NOTE

Hello fellow seeker! If you have decided to read this book, then I can guess that you are interested in and curious about the psychic world. Perhaps you are wondering exactly what (and where) it is, and how it all works.

I have been a practicing professional psychic for over thirty-five fascinating and amazing years. I see my psychic abilities as a benefaction from the Universe that must be shared with the world, and I feel privileged to have been able to witness and facilitate my clients' success in navigating life's challenges. My primary goal as a psychic is to promote hope and healing in the world, to let people know that anything is possible, and to be assured that there are *no* coincidences. It is crucial for us to realize that we are all connected to each other. Underneath the roles we play and the jobs we do, we are Spirit.

Many people express surprise when they discover that I am a psychic. I very often get the comment, "You're a psychic? You don't look like one! You're so 'normal' looking!" I have come to realize that many people have a preconceived notion of the way a psychic looks and acts. They may be expecting an eccentric, dressed in Gypsy-like garb. In reality, I am just a normal American suburbanite, not a side-show oddity. I don't entertain the idea of the Devil, monsters, vampires, goblins, or zombies. (Although, I am known for my "killer" Halloween parties!) I am the wife, the mom, or the friend you might see at the supermarket or the mall—your normal everyday next-door neighbor who just happens to have an "antenna" that can pick up and tune into phenomena on psychic airwaves.

Throughout my career, many clients have focused mainly on acquiring answers to specific questions pertaining to their own lives. However, I am often asked about what it is like to *be* psychic: what does it feels like; what do I "see" when channeling, and what are the benefits and drawbacks of my "gift?" I actually prefer not to use the word 'gift' because I want to remain humble and grateful for my intuitive abilities, and not be carried away by an inflated ego. I don't pretend to have all the answers to every question; indeed, no human knows everything, or we wouldn't be here having this human experience. In this book, I answer seekers' questions based on what I know to be true from my life experiences and through my particular "Deborah Batty Colyer filter."

Let me assure you: every story in this book actually happened and has been witnessed and verified by its principals. I honor my clients' privacy and never share their stories without their permission. In some stories I have changed names to protect my clients' privacy

Each chapter is represented by one or more of the twenty-two major tarot cards, as it relates to the chapter subject matter. Part One of this book will address the most often-asked questions. In Part Two, I will share with you my most mind-blowing, fascinating, funny and, yes, even scary experiences as a psychic. I will share with you what truths I have learned as a result of my thirty-five-year career.

I am so happy that you have decided to satisfy your curiosity by delving into these pages. I hope your journey brings you enlightenment, hope, and excitement about pursuing your own psychic adventures!

Deborah Batty Colyer

∞

FOREWORD

The following is a paper written by a student in my old neighborhood who was given a very interesting writing assignment. I think she captured the spirit (pun intended) of what I do. She has graciously allowed me to include it in this book. The following is Nikki's paper in its entirety:

When I was first assigned to interview a local folklore tale or person dealing with the paranormal, I was at a loss. Not only is my town a boring place where exciting things rarely happen, but I didn't know anybody who worked or dealt with the paranormal. I asked my mother for ideas and she told me that a lady who lived down the block from us, whom I had known for years, was a tarot card reader. *Perfect!* I thanked my mom for the helpful information and set out on my journey (just down the block) to interview this very interesting lady. Little did I know what an exciting night lay before me...

The minute I walked into her house, I felt as though I had stepped into another realm. It smelled of sweet, yet unknown aromas. There was mystical music playing softly in the background, and there was a special air to the house which I could not describe. She kindly greeted me and led me to her kitchen where the interview would take place. I was feeling a little nervous at first, not knowing what to expect throughout the course of the interview, but she was so easy and fun to talk to, that I felt right at home, and then our interview began.

I was so wrapped up in the interview that I had a difficult time recording everything. So please bear with me. Here are the things which my interview produced. Mrs. Colyer is a tarot reader, and she also teaches tarot and ways to stimulate intuition. When I asked her how the tarot cards work, she replied, "How does love work?" meaning that feeling and interpretation can be different from reader to reader. She fully believes tarot is a tool for divination (telling the future), and is used to analyze problems, clarify the decision-making process, and help you understand certain aspects of your life and, my favorite, "help the mind escape from the habitual straightjacket of logical thought."

It is believed that tarot first began in Italy as a fun game called "Tarooci." It later went underground because the church did not approve of it as a tool for divination. There are 78 cards in a deck; 22 major cards dealing with major life change, and 56 minor cards dealing with lesser mysteries of life. There are different ways of dealing the cards. Mrs. Colyer used the "Celtic Cross" which involved 11 cards. There are even different decks of cards. Each artist's rendition of the deck has a very different feeling to it, as she showed me. She preferred to use the Rider-Waite deck which is the most traditional deck. The care of the cards is also very important as she pointed out to me. The tarot cards can be wrapped in silk and "smudged." Smudging is a process in which sage or incense is burned and smudged onto the cards as she demonstrated for me.

After all of this information, I suppose Mrs. Colyer decided the best way for me to develop a full understanding of the tarot cards, would be to experience them first-hand. I must admit I was rather skeptical at first, but I proceeded with anticipation through the sample reading she was about to give me. She shuffled the cards around and then handed them to me to shuffle also. She spread the many mysterious cards on the table face down and told me choose the 11 cards that called out to me. I did as she said. She took the chosen cards from me and told me think of a question I had while she arranged them in a pattern face-up on the table. She went through each card and interpreted it for me. I was absolutely speechless. It was unthinkable that a woman I hardly knew could know such deep, personal things about me and what was occurring in my life. How she could know these little details astonished me. At one point during the reading, I became so emotional. I actually began to get choked up! It was an extremely amazing experience. She advised me on how to deal with certain problems and answered questions that I needed to know. I had forgotten all about the interview because I was so wrapped up by the reading. "The cards never lie," she told me, and I knew it was true. I went from a skeptic to an enthralled believer! After the reading, I felt as though I had a new, extremely close bond with Mrs. Colyer. One of the last notes I recorded on my interview sheet after the reading was, "It works!"

She also went on to tell me that she was a "medium," meaning that the dead speak through her. She realized she had this special gift when she was 15 and she experienced a prophetic dream. She can tap into the deceased when she wants, but sometimes they come to her as in the movie "Ghost" or "The Sixth Sense." She also told me that Abe Lincoln was actually a medium and held séances for his dead son. Lincoln also had a prophetic dream in which he saw himself being assassinated. I could probably hold another entire interview on this aspect of Mrs. Colyer alone! I never wanted to leave her house, but I knew I must. So, with a hug and a thank you, I left her mystical house where my views on things had changed drastically. I felt as if I floated home.

When I reached home and tried explaining to my family my experiences at Mrs. Colyer's house, I reminded myself of one of those people on psychic infomercials that I used to make fun of. I felt as though I had been awakened to this new and exciting world to which Mrs. Colyer introduced me. And there is still so much to learn!

Teacher's Comment:

100/100 A+

You did a great job on this, Nikki. It sounds like you had quite an experience with a remarkable woman!

∞

THE MAJOR ARCANA CARDS

The following are the twenty-two major arcana tarot cards from the Rider Waite tarot deck, along with their basic meanings. There are actually seventy-eight cards in total, but these twenty-two are the "meat and potatoes" of the deck. Through my many years of tarot reading experience I have learned that each person's interpretation of a card can vary depending on his or her own interpretive filter combined with Spirit's method of guidance.

The cards are presented in numerical order in this section, but in the body of the book they are placed within the chapter to which they most closely correlate. As is true in real life, things rarely fall in chronological order.

∞

THE FOOL.

Beginning, innocence,
spontaneity, carefree

THE MAGICIAN.

Power. skill, action
concentration

THE HIGH PRIESTESS

Intuition, higher
power, mystery

THE EMPRESS.

Femininity, nurture,
Mother Earth, nature,
birth, fertility

THE EMPEROR.

Authority, father figure,
structure, solid foundation

THE HIEROPHANT.

Conformity, tradition, religion, group identification

THE LOVERS.

Love, union, bonds,
alignment, relationships

THE CHARIOT.

Control, will power,
victory, assertion

STRENGTH.

Strength, courage,
patience, control

THE HERMIT.

Soul-searching, introspec-
tion, being alone, guidance

WHEEL of FORTUNE.

Luck, karma, destiny,
turning point

JUSTICE.

Justice, fairness,
karma, cause and effect

THE HANGED MAN.

Suspension, letting go, sacrifice, martyrdom

DEATH.

Endings, beginnings, life cycle, transition

TEMPERANCE.

Balance, moderation, patience

THE DEVIL.

Bondage, addiction, sexuality, materialism

THE TOWER.

Disaster, sudden change, revelation

THE STAR.

Hope, spirituality, renewal, inspiration

THE MOON.

Illusion, fear, insecurity, mystery

THE SUN.

Fun, warmth, love, positivity, vitality, enlightenment

JUDGEMENT.

Judgement, rebirth, inner calling

THE WORLD.

Completeness, integration, accomplishment

PART ONE

MOST COMMON QUESTIONS

Chapter One

When Did You Know You Were Psychic?

THE HIGH PRIESTESS

The High Priestess

Daughter of the moon; psychic powers;
rely on intuition rather than the intellect.

I was born in 1961 on Glenmore Street in Southwest Philadelphia, (or Philly as we call it), the stomping grounds of Rocky and Vince Papale. We lived in a densely-populated neighborhood of tiny row homes. Everybody was packed in, but instead of breeding contempt, our familiarity bred the love and warmth of a close-knit family. Everybody took care of each other, and of course, there were lots and lots of kids. We had huge kid birthday parties. I remember one with twenty-two kids! My mom would prepare an enormous party table and all of my cousins would come over. The women would drink coffee and smoke cigarettes. (Back in those days, they thought this was very glamorous.) The dads would go to work and the moms would all hang out together. There were no "Mommy and Me" classes or even preschools at that time, so we all played at each other's houses and in the street while our moms chatted with each other and looked on.

These were ladies who had generations upon generations of family tradition, customs, and continuity. They were very earthy and tuned into nature and the cycles of life. They passed on their knowledge to each subsequent generation. One of the pieces of wisdom they would pass on was what they called the "the knowing." This was a kind of understanding or deeper intuition with which they could sense what was going on beneath the surface of a person or situation. For instance, when a new person or family moved into the neighborhood, they'd come over to meet our families. After they left, the ladies would say, "Oh they're not gonna last," or "He's no good." They were almost always right. They just knew. Today we might use the term "psychic" to describe these ladies. They were just born that way. It was nothing they formally learned. As a very impressionable young girl, I simply observed them and took everything in.

One incident in particular stands out as my first real introduction to the psychic world. Our home on Glenmore Street was a tiny two-bedroom row house. My mom, dad, sister, and I all slept in the same room. (Now I know why there were only two kids!) My grandfather and uncle slept in the other bedroom. I was always scared at night. I didn't like it to be dark or silent. You might wonder how someone could be scared with four people sleeping in the same room, but I was. Perhaps deep down I had already sensed my gift and was afraid of it.

My grandmother had eight kids, and her sister had eleven. My cousins would visit frequently so there was always a lot of noise, laughter, and chaos in our house. One day, someone brought a new baby to visit. Everyone was so excited. We ran around shouting, "The new baby's here! The new baby's here!" Everyone fussed and cooed over the baby.

One of the ladies decided it was time for a diaper change. As was done in those days, they went up to a bedroom to change the baby. Mothering was innate to them. They didn't read books about it or have any special equipment such as changing tables, and they all helped each other. They were a village. They trained and taught each other, much like a tribe. She laid the baby on the bed, which was old and sagged in the middle. They were all saying things about the baby such as, "He's got his eyes," and "He's got his toes." All of the ladies were gushing. All of a sudden, I saw the bed dent down. The indentation looked as if someone was leaning on the bed. We all saw it, but none of the ladies even blinked an eye. Someone said, "Ahh, smell that pipe smoke? That's Poppy!"

My mom said, very nonchalantly and matter-of-factly, "Oh Poppy's here to see the baby." (My mom was raised by her grandparents, and called her grandfather Poppy.) I couldn't believe what I was seeing! I wanted to scream and run out of the room. I was scared to death, and they were all just laughing and chattering as if nothing unusual was happening. I thought, *Yikes, these ladies are all batshit crazy!* To them this was as natural as breathing. To me it was like something out of *Rosemary's Baby*! It was *freaky*. This was the first time I witnessed a truly psychic phenomenon.

I received my first inkling that *I* might have "the knowing" at about age thirteen when I had a dream about a little baby in a coffin. I told my mom about it, and she told me it was okay and not to worry. I didn't think she was taking me seriously, and insisted, "No, Mom, this is *really* real, not just a dream. I know the difference."

At this time, I was also having dreams in which I observed activity I could not otherwise possibly have known about. It was as if I was a piece of dust in the upper corner of a room looking down. I know now that I was astral flying and viewing the scene from the top of a room. I was having prophetic dreams and dreams in which I was leaving my body and remote viewing. When I told my mom about them, she always reassured me that it was okay and that it wasn't unnatural. I liked these dreams. I thought they were cool. But I did not like the dark dream of the baby's funeral.

The day after I dreamt of the baby's funeral, I was in my woodshop class at Collingdale High school, where, uncannily, I observed a student in my class making a small coffin. He was not making it to be used as an actual coffin but as a decoration of some sort. Even so, it was still an unbelievably creepy and an unexpected coincidence. Coming home from school that day, I saw and felt a dark presence whoosh by me. Totally upset, I ran home and told my mom. She sat me down, took my hands in hers and explained that sometimes before someone passes, a person who has "the knowing" might experience this kind of dark visitation. Mom told me that she had had "the knowing" her whole life. She made this revelation calmly, and matter-of-factly so as not to scare me.

"I don't know if I like this," I said nervously.

She replied with a soft chuckle and a wry smile, "Well it seems you don't have a choice."

A week or so later, when I came home from school, Mom said, "Come and sit down; I need to talk with you."

"What is it?" I asked.

She gently informed me that one of our cousins had given birth to a baby boy, but sadly, there were complications and he did not survive. They honored him with a memorial service that mirrored my dream. As a naive adolescent who was not yet well-versed in the dynamics of the metaphysical world, I agonized over this. I thought that my prophetic dream must have had something to do with this horrible outcome.

I sobbed to my mom, "Oh my God, could this be *my* fault?"

She reassured me that I had nothing to do with causing the baby's passing. She consoled me, saying, "You just tuned into it." That was the true beginning of my recognition of my burgeoning "gift."

∞

1960s Glenmore Street in Southwest Philly, along with a few supernatural visitors.

Fond memories in my old neighorhood.

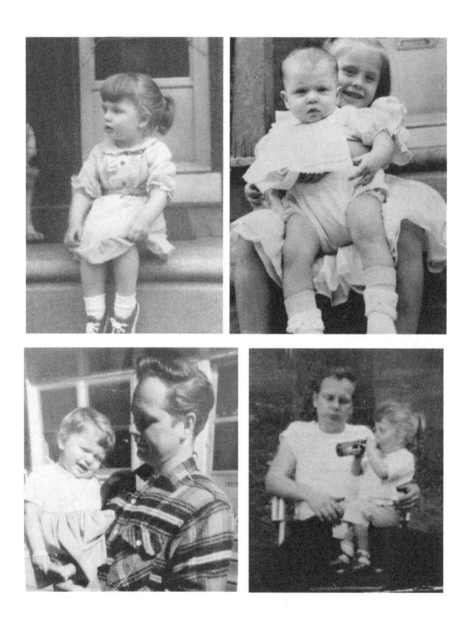

Just hangin' out...

Chapter Two

Why You and Not Me?

The Hierophant

Religion; old traditions; high priest ritual; orthodox advice; ceremony becomes gateway to higher knowledge.

Some people may ignore or deny their intuitive abilities because of their religious, cultural, or educational backgrounds, which may profess that psychic phenomena simply do not exist or are "the work of the Devil." However, I believe that religion and cultural traditions can happily coexist with and even enhance one's psychic abilities and experiences. After all, they are based on cultivating a connection and relationship with the Divine. I was raised in a family of practicing Methodists, but it was also perfectly natural to believe in psychic intuition as well. We were all in tune with nature and each other. Whatever labels we used to describe our "knowings" really didn't matter. We just accepted our "knowings" as a natural and normal aspect of life. We saw no conflict with our religion at all.

The following story is a great example of how psychic practices can exist side by side with religion:

A few years ago, a group of lovely and spunky ladies from Little Italy in South Philly booked an appointment with me to have a Maloik removed. The Maloik, or "Evil Eye" is placed on someone by another who is jealous of his or her good luck. The Maloik then manifests itself as some sort of misfortune onto the cursed person, usually some physical ailment. This can also be done involuntarily, like when you see a beautiful baby and you compliment the parent. This could be construed as envy and the parent must immediately say, "God bless her," to ward off a possible Maloik. This is because they believe that even though the compliment may have sounded sincere, its real motive was envy. The person who gives the evil eye is not necessarily evil, but does harbor jealousy.

They taught me how to remove the Maloik. I have subsequently performed the ritual successfully many times. In doing so, I have learned that this tradition is not exclusive to any one culture. This is a great example of how, even though we may come from different cultures, we can all benefit from each other's unique perspectives. It is possible to incorporate cultural traditions and educational knowledge into our lives, even if they are not included in religious doctrine or educational curriculum. We can seek the spiritual through many avenues and still have them all coexist.

Another major reason people may deny or fail to cultivate their psychic abilities is fear. Sometimes the negative stuff screams louder than the positive, which can be quite frightening. In general, experiencing deep emotions such as love, compassion, empathy, self-awareness, and grief sharpens psychic intuition.

I believe that everyone possesses psychic intuition. Most simply do not stop, be still, and listen. Everyday obligations can override the calmness, reflection, and meditation that are needed to promote psychic reception. People may believe that the song running around in their heads is just a nuisance, not a message. They ignore or tamp down a recurring "feeling" not recognizing its importance. Another way to think of it is that we are all "radio receivers." Because everyday life is so noisy and busy, or some simply do not believe in that which they cannot see, folks stubbornly dismiss any psychic intuition out of hand. Thus, their "radio receivers" are simply not tuned to the right "station."

∞

Chapter Three

Tarot Card Reading: How Does It Work?

The Hermit

Teacher, unconventional or otherwise; lighting the path; wisdom; counselor; promoting spiritual or psychological growth.

First let me say that, for me, tarot card reading is not simply about predicting the future. I try to connect with my clients in an exchange of energy and information. I see it as a privilege and a great honor to help clients find peace, comfort, and healing. I am so grateful whenever I can be an agent to help others.

I always conduct readings on an empty stomach. This enables me to focus and fully concentrate on receiving Spirit, as my body is not diverting precious energy to digestion. Drinking water also helps me, as water is a great conductor of energy. In preparation for a consultation, I white-sage the room to clear out any previous vibrations. This is a Native American ritual that involves fanning the room with smoldering sage. I also turn on a salt light to neutralize negativity, and spread crystals. Then I create a soothing and meditative atmosphere by lighting candles and putting on soft music, such as soundscapes. I never use music with lyrics because it is too distracting.

After setting the scene I meditate and state my intention for the outcome of the reading. I always appeal to Spirit to guide the consultation to the client's highest good. I ask *How can I best help them?* and *Please give me the tools I will need to bring enlightenment and comfort.*

At the beginning of the reading, I caution the client not to reveal any information at all. I let them know that they can ask any questions at the end of the session. I actually have had many clients ask me if I had researched them on the internet before their session because they were so utterly astounded as to how much I could tell them about themselves. I assure them that it is absolutely against my ethics to perform any prior research on clients.

I then explain how the card reading process works. I shuffle the cards, telling my brain to turn on. Then the client shuffles the cards while thinking about what he or she wants to know and is interested in tapping into. It could be two questions or twenty. If they have no specific questions then I let them know that the reading will be for their highest good.

The more the client is stressed, the harder it is to connect. In the first few minutes of every consultation, my goal is to get on the client's "spiritual frequency." The key to a successful reading is encouraging the client to be open-minded, relaxed, and to abandon any preconceived notions. I never read anyone who doesn't want to be read because their fear bubbles to the surface creating a self-fulfilling prophecy.

Of the many card layouts, the eleven-card Celtic Cross Spread most resonates with me. The symbols, numbers, and colors combine to form the thread of information which begins to flow. It starts visually at first, and then becomes multi-sensory. When I'm "in the zone," information flows easily. I like to call this "threading the needle." At times, it will come to the point when I begin to channel empathically, and no cards are needed to receive information.

As I mentioned before, I make it a point never to ask questions of the client that would reveal to me any personal information. I need to have confidence in what I see in the cards—even if it doesn't make sense to me at first. I will often receive symbols or images that don't fit together, only to later realize that they do indeed fit together in very meaningful ways. I will explain the details and ask the client if he or she understands. Most of the time they confirm that they do understand. I don't need to know what the story is, unless it pertains to further questions. I don't feel the need to probe any further. I follow their lead when I read because it may be pertinent to putting the pieces together. However, sometimes they don't want to "go there" because it's a painful memory. This is the Universe's way of letting them know that I'm authentic. For example, I read a woman whose cards indicated that she had married the same man three times. I thought surely I must be wrongly interpreting something. *How could this be?*

"Your marriage situation boggles my mind," I told her. "The cards say that you married the same guy three times!"

She grinned, "That's because I did!"

In another client's reading, I kept getting male and female cards. I was mystified. At the risk of upsetting my client I said, "You're confusing me. The cards are indicating that you were born with both male and female parts."

Her mouth dropped open in stunned surprise. Staring at me in wonder, she said, "Wow, you're good…"

Here again was confirmation that I need to follow my gut even if it doesn't make sense to me at the time. If a client says, "I knew that already," during a reading, it validates my authenticity.

Commonly during a reading, various deceased loved ones may step forward asking to communicate. I cannot initiate this because it happens organically. It cannot be forced on demand. I will expand on this topic further in the next chapter.

After the hundreds and hundreds of readings I have done, the most shocking revelation I have had is how many people have been abused and assaulted in some way. Sadly, it is much more common than people may think.

Towards the end of the reading, I offer to answer any questions. More often than not the client's questions have already been answered during the reading. Even if they were skeptical and/or stoic at first, the walls seem to come down and they feel safe to express themselves without being judged. In essence, we are healing each other through an intense, pure, human-to-human connection. This is my validation that, as humans, we are all connected.

The beauty of card reading is that it is the great equalizer. No matter what a person's occupation, financial status, or cultural background, their daily social mask dissolves and the healing work begins. This takes time, concentration, energy, and patience. I am compassionate and loving regardless of who my client is: hit-man or celebrity. The surface is all stripped away in the moment. It is the meeting of souls with no judgment. I am always pleased when clients walk away with a more enlightened perspective on their personal issues and are introduced to previously unrealized possibilities.

∞

Tarot card reading; enjoying my craft.

Chapter Four

As a Medium, Exactly What Do You See, Feel, and Hear when Channeling?

Death

Not necessarily a physical death; letting go; transformation; dying in order to be reborn; an ending; the cycles that constantly occur in nature.

I believe that death is simply another dimension. After they cross over, some souls communicate, some go away, some visit. I cannot command specific spirits to show up. I can only channel those who choose to communicate with the client.

Often during sessions, my tarot card reading evolves into mediumship. Spirit wants to connect with my client. A sure sign of Spirit arriving is when I feel chills on my left side from head to toe. The presence will not leave because it wants so badly for me to acknowledge it. I might hear a song and ask the client if it has personal meaning. It invariably means something special and specific to that particular client. Even with my eyes open, I will often see symbols or images that play like a mini-movie in my mind's eye.

For example, when I describe a symbol or image to the client such as a birthmark or tattoo, the client will usually confirm in amazement that the person who crossed over indeed had a tattoo of that symbol or image. Sometimes meanings can be obscure. I may not know what a symbol or image represents, but I have to trust that what's coming through will mean something to the client. When I get it right, I will feel chills again. It's as if Spirit gets excited that I'm getting it right.

On occasion, when I channel, I experience emotions that I haven't undergone in my own life. I may experience waves of crushing sadness and despair, as well as heightened euphoria and joy, depending on the clients' current life circumstances.

When the spirit of someone who has passed comes through, I can actually *feel* its personality. As they were over here, so they are over there. I will get a sense of the characteristics of the spirit whether it is protective, humorous, loving, fearful, etc. I once had a client whose father was a "player" here and was still the same flirt over there. I even got a wink! My client drew the King of Cups card, reversed, which indicates a perpetual lover.

I might also see an energy ball at a height akin to the spirit's age and relationship to the client. A grandfather would be at the tallest height, a father lower, and a son still lower. Sometimes the spirit will stand behind the client or on the floor indicating a pet that has crossed over.

Happily, most of the time, spirits appear healthy and younger than when they passed. Spirits can even communicate in different languages. I once had client who was an accomplished karate master. During his reading, a spirit began speaking to me in a foreign language that I didn't understand. I asked the client if he knew anyone who would try to communicate in a foreign language. He confirmed in astonishment, that it was his former dojo, who had crossed over years prior.

I have been an instructor at several Pennsylvania institutions. Among them are Ridley Adult School and the renowned Parastudy organization in Chester Heights.

The old Victorian mansion which houses Parastudy has been said to be haunted by several ghostly entities. According to the Parastudy website, there is said to be the ghost of an old man on the outside property grounds and the ghost of a young boy inside the house on the stairs. The ghosts of two women are said to haunt the third floor: one is sickly. The other is a nurse.

When I went to Parastudy to interview for an instructor position, I was introduced quite quickly into the world of the spirits that occupy the property. The moment I stepped on to the property, I felt a ghostly aura that hung heavy in the atmosphere.

By the time the interview was over, it was evening. Parastudy's location is out in the countryside. Without city lights, the nights are very, very dark. As I left the building and made my way to my car in the pitch blackness, I heard the low, raspy whispers of what seemed to be hundreds of people. Normally this doesn't worry me, but in this instance, there were so many. The hairs on the back of my neck rose, and I'm not embarrassed to say, I was a bit unnerved, having never experienced something this intense. I jumped into my cherished, brand-new Acura as quickly as possible, and made a beeline for home.

That night, I tossed and turned in a fitful slumber. A horrible headache developed, forcing me to go to the bathroom for some Tylenol and a glass of water. In the process, I looked out my window to check on my new car, parked at the front curb.

My jaw dropped to my chest when I saw that someone was sitting in the front passenger seat! I rubbed my eyes and looked again to make sure I wasn't dreaming. Sure enough, there was an elderly lady occupying the front passenger seat, her face in profile. But more amazingly, the woman's body was crystal clear! She was transparent and dressed in a flowing, amorphous, nightgown-like garment.

Shocked, I realized that I had picked up a hitchhiker spirit at the Parastudy mansion. My thoughts raced—*Should I wake my family? Would they believe me?* I wanted somebody to witness this.

I walked away for about twenty minutes or so, then looked out the window again. There she was! Still in the car! She wouldn't look at me. She simply sat facing forward looking lost and confused. I got a strong feeling that she needed to be returned back to the familiar surroundings of the Parastudy mansion.

The next morning, I sprinkled some salt on the front passenger seat, cracked the window a bit so that she would be able to leave the car at will, and headed back to the Parastudy campus to teach my first class. Along the way, I explained to her that she needed to go home, and that was where I was taking her. I was not completely certain this strategy would work, but I figured I'd give it a shot.

My first Parastudy tarot class consisted of mostly teachers, who were already deeply immersed in the paranormal arts, and full of questions and suggestions.

I was a bit drained after the class, as I had been experiencing back trouble recently. Several of the class members volunteered to perform Reiki, a form of energy healing, on me.

We adjourned to the third-floor therapy room where I lay, eyes closed, on the Reiki table. As the students circled the table performing their healing ritual, I sensed an older woman's energy in the room. She moved to different parts of the room as the Reiki practitioners moved around the table. I thought it odd because this energy was distinctly different and separate from the rest of the group. I didn't know whose energy it was.

I didn't think much more about it because I enjoyed my Reiki therapy session so much and was thrilled about the results. My back felt wonderful, my energy restored. I drove home happy about such a successful and enjoyable evening.

Late into the night, I awoke, and went to the window once again to check on my car. I let out a deep sigh of relief when I saw that it was empty.

∞

Parastudy in Chester Heights, PA

Chapter Five

Does Everything You Predict Come True?

What About Bad News?

THE TOWER.

The Tower

Forced change that which needs to be changed is changed; the breaking down of existing forms to make way for something new; rebuild on a firm foundation; changes beliefs and notions you've had your entire life; chaos preceding liberation.

Contrary to some people's beliefs, psychics aren't "know-it-alls." We do not possess all the answers to all of life's mysteries. My advice to you is to run fast in the opposite direction from any psychic who claims otherwise. The cards don't always provide specific answers, but when the same cards keep coming up, I pay attention and simply read what I see. I do not feel that it's a cop-out when I don't know the answers, as Spirit only gives me what it wants the client to know.

I always try to stay positive in readings but sometimes clients' lives are not on a positive cycle. They know it too, but can't see when or how it will change. I try to provide guidance, but I have no power to change the future. I can only predict. If a client's cards indicate a negative downward spiral, Spirit will suggest alternative solutions that the client might not otherwise have considered. I counsel my clients that the cards' predictions are not written in stone. The future is always subject to change.

Across the board, the most common question from clients is, "Will I ever be happy?" My answer is that it is up to them. I can provide guidance and discuss the signs, but in truth, life is about free will and free choice. The answers *really* are all up to you.

∞

Chapter Six

You Say There Are No Coincidences.

What Do You Mean?

Wheel of Fortune

Unexpected change; advancement for
better; gambling; synchronicity.

When I say that there are no coincidences, I mean that certain signs show up in our lives serendipitously and usually for our greater good. Normally they come to us as signs of love and encouragement to let us know that we are on our right paths, and that we are loved. These signs are special and unique to each of us. We need only to learn to recognize them and apply them to our situations. The following are a few examples of how these signs have showed up in my life.

The Buck Stops Here

In the early days of our relationship, my husband, like many of my friends and acquaintances, believed that *I* believed I was psychic but still remained skeptical about the whole "psychic thing." I can think of two instances that turned my husband-the-skeptic into a believer.

One day, we driving along some very twisting and winding roads on our way to a family reunion at French Creek park. I was feeling a bit uneasy because my speed-loving husband was going a bit too fast for this rollercoaster road. In a surreal moment, I had a vision of a deer around the next curve. I screamed, "Stop!" at the top of my lungs. My husband slammed on the brakes just as we rounded the curve. To the amazement of all, there before us stood a huge buck that had just stepped into the roadway. My two little boys in the back seat stared at me wide-eyed and said, "Whoa, Mom!" My husband gaped at me in shock, and I remember thinking, *Well, he believes me now!*

A Friend in Need

Years ago, when Gary worked for a major electronics company, he and his friend Ron carpooled to work together. When Ron left that job to go to work in a chemical plant, they didn't carpool anymore. As a consequence, they didn't see very much of each other. A few years later, I had a dream of Ron in the hospital. In the dream, he was carrying a chemical-type drum container. I then saw him in the hospital badly burned around his neck and arms, screaming in pain. When I awoke, I asked Gary if he had heard from Ron lately. He answered that he hadn't because they had lost touch.

Feeling haunted by my dream, I suggested to Gary that he might want to get in touch with Ron to see if he was okay. I revealed to him my disturbing dream.

Within weeks Ron called from the hospital and explained that he had gotten chemical burns from an accident at work. I felt bad that I didn't trust the dream enough to have warned him.

We visited Ron in the hospital. Thankfully, he was okay. When I told him about my dream, he was noncommittal, but it sure made Gary a believer!

217:   Out of The Mouths of Babes

"I love you 217" was a phrase my mother said often to me as a child. For years I never questioned where it came from. We only knew that it meant "the most love you could possibly express." My parents married young in 1955. Within a few weeks of the ceremony, my father was shipped out to France to serve in the armed forces. He was gone for two years. As newlyweds deeply in love, one can imagine the longing they felt for each other. On every love letter, photo, and package Mom wrote, "I love you 217." Dad wrote the same to her on all of his return correspondence. It became a tradition within our family to use Mom's number of love and affection.

One day while still a child, I asked Mom, "Why do you love us 217?" She explained that the phrase originated in her childhood with her youngest sister, Shirley (my sister Shirley's namesake). Mom had a big family with a lot of siblings.

One day her baby sister said, "Alma May I love you 217."

My mother, curious, replied, "Why 217?"

With the guilelessness and exuberance of her young years, Aunt Shirley replied, "Cause it's the biggest number I know!"

The phrase stuck and became a tradition that is still used within our family to this day. Aunty Shirley's daughter, Dawn and her husband Pete, actually named their wildly successful business "Two17 Photography and Cinema" in honor of our loving family phrase.

The number 217 uncannily pops up during happy times and sad as a reminder to us to love deeply, with all our hearts and souls. It shows up like a rainbow, or a penny on heads, or a feather, as a sign. When I see it out in the world, such as on a license plate, an address, or a marquee, I know she is sending her love. I always smile and say, "Thanks, Mom."

On the day of Mom's funeral service, the Universe was working its mysterious ways once more. At the service, my cousins who had been very close to Mom, presented beautiful, heartfelt tributes to their cherished "Aunt May."

My cousin Kim called me shortly after the service to tell me that she had stopped off at the local Wawa to grab a hoagie on her way home. She took a number at the deli counter but never looked at it, as she was still reeling from the emotional funeral service and grieving for Aunt May.

A shout from the deli counter clerk broke through her reverie, "Now serving 217! Now serving 217!"

She slowly opened her hand, not even surprised to see the number 217, and thought, "Of course it's *my* number. What other number could it have possibly been? Aunt May had conveyed her love to Kim from beyond.

Is it a coincidence that this book is being published in 2017? I'll leave it to you to decide...

∞

Mom, Aunt Shirley, and Auntie,

the original 217 sisters.

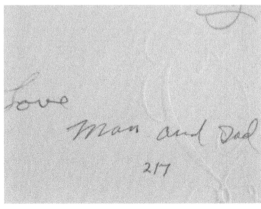

Chapter Seven

Why Haven't You Won the Lottery? And the Ever Popular: What Color Is My Underwear?

Temperance

Conscience and unconscious come together; compromise; good mixture; obtain the right combination before best result; flexible in attitude.

First, let me emphasize that I am not the one creating the information for my client. I am merely a channeler. The information for the client comes *through* me not *from* me. If Spirit wishes to communicate with me for issues in my life, I receive signs, symbols and messages of Spirit's choosing, not mine. I cannot conjure answers at will even for myself.

Second, the curse of being a good card reader is that you tend to see for others but can't always see for yourself. I go to trusted psychics for extra insight into my life situations, much like a psychologist would see another psychologist for therapy rather than practice self-treatment.

Occasionally, the same card in the same position comes up many times throughout many consecutive readings. When this occurs, I realize that Spirit is playing a cosmic joke. It turns out that the meaning is for me, not the client. A dropped card or a card that flies from the deck when shuffled could signal the same. If a card is missing from a tarot reader's deck, then it can be a red flag to the reader who owns the deck to pay attention to that card. It is Spirit's way of refocusing me, for I am usually concentrating on my clients, my family, and my friends rather than myself.

People sometimes try to get cheeky with me and will ask something to the effect of, "If you're so psychic, then what color underwear am I wearing?" Honestly, if I really wanted to spend the client's time and my energy on this kind of question, I could successfully answer, but I really don't want to waste the client's money on a parlor trick and cheapen the experience. In a case like this, I usually make a lighthearted joke—something like, "Oh this is a trick question because you're not wearing any, right?" Then we both have a little laugh and get on with the business at hand.

∞

Chapter Eight

Is Being a Professional Psychic Fun and Easy?

The Fool

Be open to adventure that is coming
your way; childlike innocence.

I enjoy being a psychic for so many reasons, but like any profession, there are ups and downs. There are fun times, feelings of validation, pleasure knowing I am helping people, and feeling a true connection to the Universe.

However, I also have to deal with critics, skeptics, and yes, even some ridicule at times. There is also the emotional drain and burn-out that comes with working too long and too hard, especially with the bereaved, the depressed, and what I call "psychic vampires." Psychic vampires monopolize conversations, talking fast, and usually over other people. They have few, if any, boundaries or filters. When you walk away from them, you feel drained and exhausted.

Oftentimes at social events when it is revealed that my occupation is a psychic, the reaction is either one of amazement and further questions or scoffing and dismissal, as if no such thing could exist. Some become distant because they fear I am reading their minds. Either way it is usually a strong reaction. Some grab my hand hoping to touch the magic. Others just turn and walk away. Some take it further, diving in with their questions as if I'm a doctor at a cocktail party.

People like me who are psychic and intuitive often have anxiety because they feel *everything*. When I am reading someone and I feel that what I am about to say will make them cry, I feel like I'm going to cry first. Unknowingly, they send the feeling to me first. Then I know what's coming. It is a both a blessing and a curse. There are times when I don't want to know or feel, but cannot shut it off. Some psychics say that they can turn it on and off, but I'm not one of them.

In the early years of my career, I worked as a party clown while I was building my following as a psychic and medium. Most people would think that these professions would be very different from each other, but they are alike in many ways.

Being a clown, like card reading, is very grounding, but it can also be very draining. I made it a point to never work above my audience. I always sat on the floor with the children making sure that I was addressing them on their level. Kids are very honest, open, free, and loving. They are also high vibrating and energy-filled beings. I usually performed for an hour at an event. After that hour, even though very tired, I still reveled in the intangible energy exchange between my small charges and myself. That is the true magic.

One day after a child's birthday party, my mom and I went shopping. I got to talking with a sales lady at one of the stores and somehow what I did for a living came up. I told her I was a card reader and a children's party clown. She asked which was more draining. My mom and I looked at each other and laughed, because my exhaustion from both had become an issue recently. Just as she asked the question, all the power in the store went out. The Universe in its metaphorical way was acknowledging that my energy was becoming totally drained.

At one time I was doing so many readings that I started to burn out. There was too much energy going out and not enough coming in. One night, I felt extremely emotionally and mentally exhausted. I lay on my bed reading *Sacred Space*. My niece, Tori, who had been visiting hopped up onto the bed beside me. I told her I was writing in my journal asking Spirit to give me a sign as to why I felt so sick and tired all the time, and what I should do about it. As we chatted, the light bulb in my bedside lamp popped loudly and startled us. As it turned out, the part of book I was reading was about electricity. We had a great laugh because the book said that overloaded circuits means too much energy is going out and not enough is coming in. If that wasn't a sign for me, I don't know what else it could have been! Sometimes, if you ask the question, you will get an answer. To ease my stress, I began meditation classes and cut back a little bit on the number of readings for a while to recharge my batteries.

∞

My past days as Bubbles the Clown.

PART TWO

MOST MEMORABLE

PSYCHIC EXPERIENCES

Chapter Nine

Future Hubby

Emperor

Strong; left brained; greatest strength is his willpower and courage; alpha male.

I am so very lucky to have had a loving, caring, and very adventurous mother. She occasionally had psychics over to read for her friends. One memorable psychic couple was Reverend Jacob and Jules who performed readings together. One read palms, the other cards. One night my mother had a last-minute cancellation so I was going to be allowed to take her friend's place.

At 14 years old, I was overjoyed to be included with her friends. I was so excited. It was like graduating from the kids' table! I was rarely even allowed in my parents' bedroom. This is where the private readings would take place. This was a double treat. I was intrigued and curious to peek behind the veil.

The room was glowing with flickering candlelight. I made my way to the card table that was set up on the large oval braided rug. There was an old-fashioned parlor feel to the room, right down to the wooden platform rocker.

I sat down at the card table between the two readers. Jules took my hand and drizzled a tear-drop of oil into my palm. He massaged it in, and to my amazement all the lines became three dimensional. I didn't even know I had that many lines on my palm. It was like going from the city to the country, where all of a sudden you can see the millions of stars in the sky that you couldn't see before because of the city lights.

Jacob began reading the tarot cards. Going back and forth between the two readers, my future began to unfold. The two together were so in sync. They were powerful vessels with a rhythmic way of each telling the future in a calm and comfortable manner. Even at that tender age, I knew they drew their information from a higher source.

At the time, I couldn't have imagined how pivotal this reading would become in my life's development as a reader. I will share with you three predictions that were eerily accurate.

The first is that Jacob and Jules validated what I had already suspected: that I had mystical gifts of my own. They assured me that I would grow into them in time. My heart pounded! My budding experiences so far had foreshadowed this moment. It was so encouraging to have it confirmed by experienced professionals.

They also told me I would be in a car accident in my teen years and, while I was alarmed, they reassured me I would survive it. I did indeed survive a car crash that very summer.

Lastly, they cryptically told me that there was an orange sports car in my future. "You will marry the guy with the orange sports car," they said. This puzzled me because I was just friends with Gary, (the man I would end up marrying) at the time, and I had designs on a boy with a green Nova. Gary's older brother owned an orange sports car, which was his prized possession. Unbeknownst to Gary, he would end up owning his brother's 1969 "Big Bad Orange" AMC Javelin. Need I say more?

∞

Mr. and Mrs. Colyer tie the knot in Collingdale, PA September, 1979.

1969 Big Bad Orange Javelin

Chapter Ten

Inipi

The Star

Nature's healing; the miracle you hoped for;
retreat; identification with all of humanity;
hopes fulfilled.

I have always been interested in and open to alternative ways of cultivating spiritual growth and enhancing my intuitive abilities. Among my past adventures, I studied the Native American Inipi, also known as the Native American Sweat Lodge. This is an ancient Native American purification rite through which participants seek spiritual rebirth, a miracle, or the fulfillment of a prayer. Each seeker attends for unique and personal reasons.

The Inipi has had some bad press in the past, but when done correctly with the right safety measures in place, it can be transformative. I explored this experience during a time of great tumult and personal stress. I was particularly concerned about my younger son, Nicholas, who had just been diagnosed with Attention Deficit Disorder at the age of six. Nicky had been a traumatic-birth baby who came into the world feet first with the umbilical cord around his neck. After an emergency Cesarean Section, the doctor told us that his birth had been a very close call. My theory is that this traumatic birth contributed to his later challenges in cognitive processing.

Shortly after Nicky's diagnosis, I decided to participate in a sweat lodge ceremony to ask Spirit to help my son with his struggles. I attended this event with an open mind but, indeed, had to step way out of my comfort zone. It was an extremely intense experience that required mental, emotional, and physical discomfort. The premise behind this profound ritual is that one must sacrifice to gain.

In preparation for the ceremony, we fasted all day. We heated the large stones to be used inside the Inipi, an igloo-shaped dome, which we would enter at some point. While the stones heated, we made prayer ties representing our deceased loved ones and prayed for spiritual, not material blessings.

Some hours later, we entered the Inipi and hung our prayer ties. We sat crossed-legged in a circle in the dirt with nothing between us and Mother Earth. A group member ladled water on the blazing hot rocks creating plumes of wafting steam. My nose began to run, and I started sweating profusely. Only the glowing rocks broke the darkness. The two Native Americans in attendance began to sing in their tribal language. Each group member expressed their purpose and intention aloud. The heat became intense, and the real sacrifice began. It quickly got to the point that I felt it was too unbearably hot to endure. Even though I was extremely uncomfortable and unsure, the will to cure my son overcame my anxiety.

Native American spirits began whipping around inside of the Inipi. One said to me telepathically, *You're the white man! What are you doing here? This is not your culture!*

I answered in my head, *I care about my son! I'm willing to embrace any spiritual assistance!*

The mood in the Inipi shifted. I felt the acceptance of the spirits. They communicated to me that it was okay that I was there, and I would be permitted to sacrifice in my longing to heal my son.

Something spiritual had transpired which reinforced the fact that this ritual did have a deep meaning.

The ceremony concluded with an au naturel cleansing dip in the cool waters of the nearby creek, followed by a re-nourishing pot luck celebratory feast at the main house. In my malaise, I bypassed the dip in the creek and headed toward the house alone to process what had just happened to me.

After the completion of the Inipi, I headed back home to my Sunday night routine of household chores and domestic responsibilities. As I was doing laundry in the basement, bubbly six-year-old Nicholas came b-bopping down the stairs. He had always been super-curious, and his questions came like rapid fire:

"How was your Indian thing, Mom? What was that Indian thing you did? Whadja do? Whadja do?"

I told him that it went fine, and that we sat in a circle and sang songs.

"Oh, like this?" he replied and broke into a Native American song that I had never heard him sing before. Incredibly, he sang the whole song—every verse! Chills erupted all over my body and I burst out crying!

"Where did you learn that song?" I asked in amazement.

"Oh, a long time ago in kindergarten," he replied.

The spirits had heard!

I knew in my heart they had heard my plea. I decided to not stress so much about what Nicky's future would hold. I felt calm relief as I handed my worries over to the Universe. Today, Nicholas is in his thirties, married and very accomplished. He is a highly-successful executive in charge of enterprise security in a prominent and respected security consulting company.

Another important take-away from this experience for me was that I realized sometimes our worries chronically eat away the precious time we could be using to revel in the joy and blessings in our lives.

∞

Chapter Eleven

The Golden Cocoon

The Empress

Great mother; goddess; the nurturer;
she creates a loving nest for her family.

The moment the woman walked through my door, I felt her pain and sorrow. There was such a great heaviness, and I knew something really terrible had happened. More and more as I read her, I realized that she had probably lost a child. This is the worst read— the worst pain. In readings like this, I can actually physically and emotionally experience the pain of a person who had to endure that situation, even though I have not personally been through a similar trauma. I didn't know what it was like to lose a child, but in that moment, I was living my client's deep despair. It's so surreal to feel something you've never personally experienced first-hand.

As the reading progressed, she sorrowfully relayed to me that she had lost a child in a car accident. However, her anguish extended beyond her loss. She wanted clarification as to exactly what the circumstances of the crash were, because there had been conflicting accounts. I didn't know the whole story but I sensed that it involved a need to clear her daughter of fault. I felt that the daughter was a good girl and was being held responsible for something she didn't do, so there had been a double injustice. I told her, "The cards say it looks as though your daughter will be cleared of any blame." I then felt a sudden, spreading warmth, indicating that her daughter wished to communicate. She wanted to thank her mom for believing in and supporting her.

For me, when a reading is over, it is usually over. I try to shut down the psychic side of myself and get on with my day. But this particular reading stuck with me as I went about my daily routine. I felt so heartbroken for this mother and her daughter. It all weighed very heavily upon me. Doubtful thoughts kept popping into my head. I began questioning my life calling. I wondered if it was ethical to accept a person's money when she was suffering so badly. Morally it didn't feel right. I had wanted to help the woman, but did I? I started to wonder if I should continue to read cards at all. I was so upset that I didn't know if I wanted to do this anymore. I would never want to take advantage of someone's heartache and pain. When people suffer such a devastating loss they may feel broken and desperate for answers. I had been reading cards for the better part of three decades, and here I was agonizing over the legitimacy of my life's purpose. I felt myself asking out loud, "Universe should I be doing this? Am I doing good or harm?"

That very night my client's daughter came to me in a dream:

> In my dream, a young beautiful girl comes to me. In her hands, she is holding golden thread. She begins wrapping me and twirling me in the golden thread. The feeling in the dream is so euphoric that I feel a rush of warmth from head to toe as she spins me in gold.

I woke up crying, but felt renewed and reassured that I was helping people and was indeed on my life's correct path. In this dream, I felt love from someone I had never known. In essence, she was telling me to keep reading cards. I was just about to quit, but her spirit was urging me to continue on.

As a rule of principle and ethics, I do not initiate contact with clients. I let them seek me out if they feel the need. But this experience was so profound, I felt absolutely compelled to talk to her mother. Because this urging would not let up, I gave in and called her.

"I never call people like this," I explained, "but I wanted you to know that your daughter came to me last night. Your daughter hugged me and hugged me and spun me in gold."

She began to cry. Through her tears, she said, "That was so my daughter."

Then I knew it was real and right. What I was doing did have merit. It really was helping other people. My client and I both knew without a doubt there had been true communication with her daughter. It was an experience of grace and healing.

∞

Chapter Twelve

Three Amazing Dreams

The Moon

Prophetic dreams; doorway to the unknown; fear; lunacy; unconscious; in dream state; flashes of past lives visits.

There are different types of dreams. We may experience "regurgitation" dreams in which the unconscious mind is simply processing recent events. In reunion dreams we reunite with loved ones who have passed over. A prophetic dream could be a warning of danger or a harbinger of good things to come. Astral travel is not truly a dream, but an experience where the soul leaves the body and travels to different locations throughout the world and the universe. Out-of-body remote viewing is an experience in which we may witness an event while asleep as it is actually occurring in real life.

I have had each type of dream many times. On the following pages are the dreams that stand out as some of the most impactful and profound I have ever experienced.

Dream Walking in Ireland

I had reached another bad burnout period and was again doubting my career calling. I had been reading cards almost nonstop and sleeping badly, if at all. Once again, I began to wonder if it was all worth it and if I was doing any good in the world. Once again, I begged Spirit to show me a sign that I was indeed on my correct path.

Spirit graciously answered me with a comforting dream:

> *In this dream, I am walking in verdant green field among ancient buildings and headstones. I have never been to Ireland, but somehow, I know that this is where I am.*
>
> *As I wander among the headstones, I see that the information on the headstones has been worn away over many, many years. A great sadness washes over me as I realize that these souls may be forgotten. As I lovingly run my hands over each headstone, I see in my mind's eye, a mini movie depicting the person's life from birth to death. Among them are a seamstress, a farmer, a blacksmith, and many more.*
>
> *At light-speed I run to each and every headstone touching one and then the next to view each life movie. Each life is unique and special. I observe how each one lived and how each one died right down to the smallest details of their lives. Their deaths ran the gamut from sickness to accident to murder.*
>
> *Suddenly I realize in the dream that I am able to help those who passed over connect with and be remembered by their loved ones.*

I awoke from the dream feeling calm and happy, reassured that I was on my correct path. All of my doubts had been erased. I was being told by Spirit was telling me once again that what I was doing was okay, and that I was contributing to the greater good of the world.

As in any profession, we need validation now and then to keep on keeping on...

Tsunami

One of the most impactful prophetic dreams I have ever experienced predicted the devastating Indian Ocean tsunami of 2004:

I'm in Africa. The colors of the plains and the sky are intense and vivid. I have never witnessed any of this in real life, as I've never physically been to Africa. I'm basking in the beauty of the colors and sensations around me when suddenly the vibrant colors change to dark, swirling, black clouds. The feeling in the dream turns ominous. I am wondering in panic what is happening. There are no trees on the African plain, only dry grasses. There is nowhere to seek shelter. I feel the vibrations of a thunderous pounding. I hear a growing roar. Daylight disappears instantly into darkness. I'm panicked. Where do I run?

The noise grows louder and louder. Then I see what looks like dust or smoke rising from the ground. I taste the dirt and sand. I look up to see a stampede of elephants, fear evident on their panicked faces. They are running from something.

Birds are flocking in great flying clouds. I start to run but know that there's no way in Hell I will outrun the elephants. I lay on the ground in a fetal position. An odd thought runs through my mind: How crazy is it that my obituary will say that I died in an elephant stampede?

The elephants run over me but do not hurt me. I realize I'm not in pain—I didn't die.

I woke up sweat-soaked, my heart pounding. I knew instantly that something really big was going to happen in the world, which would have to do with Mother Nature. I had no idea what it would be, but I knew the dream was not a personal message for me but rather a prophetic dream having to do with the larger world.

To my amazement, mere days later, the Indian Ocean Tsunami wreaked its havoc.

My Ship

Another memorable prophetic dream occurred at a time in my life when I felt stuck and frustrated. I wanted to move out of my tiny house to a larger one in my dream neighborhood. There was no way we could afford to move at that time. On top of that, I had just lost a dear friend and was in mourning. One night, when I was feeling depressed and out of hope, I had this dream:

I walk to the end of my street and come upon a gigantic ship. It is pristine and shiny and beautiful. I am feeling euphoric. I suddenly realize that the ship is larger than the tops of the houses. I realize that this dream is telling me that my "ship is about to come in."

I woke up feeling happy and positive, and knew that something wonderful was going to happen soon. Within days, my husband Gary received a huge promotion which allowed us to buy our dream house where we still live happily today.

∞

Chapter Thirteen

The Shed

The Magician

Original and skilled; helps us learn about ourselves;
look for the spiritual element in everyday life.

Although I usually conduct tarot readings in one-on-one sessions, I occasionally read at special events. One day, I received a call from a woman requesting my services at a group party. Nothing unusual came up during our conversation until she told me that I would be conducting the readings in her shed. *Shed?* Now, I have read cards in bedrooms, family rooms, basements, and attics because of the need for private space —but a shed? This was a new one. I asked the client if the shed was heated. After all, it was October and very chilly. She told me not to worry and assured me that this shed was a very *special* place.

On the day of the event, when I arrived at the house, it seemed to be like any other normal house. I didn't notice anything out of the ordinary at all. My client, Dottie, greeted me warmly and led me to the back yard where the shed was located. With a bit of trepidation, I followed, not at all sure what I had gotten myself into.

As we entered the back yard, my senses began to tingle and a rush of warmth coursed through me. I felt as though I had been instantaneously transported to a different world. This shed was no big box store aluminum contraption. This shed was absolutely charming and unique, with a personality all its own. It was cabin-like; rustic and quaint. It looked like it belonged somewhere in Arizona, surely not in the burbs of Philly.

This shed was a work of art, painstakingly and lovingly built. It had been constructed with hand-laid stonework arranged in gorgeous mosaic patterns, culminating in an exquisitely crafted masterpiece.

The huge heavy wooden door creaked with age as my client opened it and invited me in. Upon entering this amazing space, I was inundated with the psychometric vibrations of love and happiness radiating from the décor. There were distinctive and whimsical objet d'art and unusual items that the owners had collected during their world travels, as well as tidbits gifted to them by friends. The ceiling was artistically draped with an old parachute and brass-tipped airplane propeller from 1916. Everywhere I looked there was something different and unique to look at. The aura and scent inside the shed was reminiscent of life-long friendships and days gone by. Each decorative item was a psychometric treasure radiating love and joy.

I later learned the origin of "The Shed." It had been built by hand from the ground up by my client's significant other, Paul, a master stone mason. Its construction had been a labor of love and passion for his craft. The building itself was made with ancient reclaimed cypress wood from Silvestri's Pennsylvania mushroom house. The mosaic on the exterior is comprised of leftovers from his many stone mason jobs. Paul created the shed to include the memories of the life he had successfully and lovingly built using his stone masonry skills.

The Shed's history actually harkens back even further in time. Paul told me that he had been taught as a young man by a master stone mason straight from the "Old Country" of Italy who passed down to him generations of skills and knowledge. He was the "real deal" right down to his penchant for eating lunch outside on the hill of the construction site and taking a midday "riposo." This is certainly not an American custom, but he was such a skilled expert that no one really minded.

I read in the shed a couple of times a year. I always enjoy its charm and uniqueness. I'm so happy to be able to visit this little piece of paradise, tucked away from the ordinary, to work my craft. It is a privilege to work my magic in a magical space.

∞

Chapter Fourteen

Never Say Never

The Lovers

Romance; sexual desire.

A few years after Gary and I were married, we moved to Ridley Park, PA. We settled in to raise our sons in a charming Cape Cod house adorned with dormer windows and window boxes sporting colorful blooms. Many of the homes in Ridley Park are beautiful, large, rambling Victorians designated as historical landmarks. The town itself is an anachronism reminiscent of the 1950s, with its walkable downtown and town center, complete with a town clock that could have been straight out the movie, ***Back to the Future.***

During those years, I had a regular Tuesday night tarot card reading gig at the Gas Light restaurant located at the Ridley Park train station. Of all of the venues at which I have worked over the years, the Gas Light is my very favorite. It has a cozy, elegant, hometown ambiance, right down to its lace tablecloths and stained-glass windows.

The Gas Light has a rich and storied history. It is constructed almost entirely of wood, festival windows, and other items rescued from homes, schools and churches of Old Ridley Park. The old photos on the walls depict the fascinating history of the town. It was built in the late 1920s as a plumbing, heating, and roofing business. Subsequently, it became a gas station in the late 1930s, and then Gus's Garage in the 1950s. Many believe that Gus' friendly ghost visits frequently. I cannot dispute the theory as I have been there many times after closing, packing up my tarot reading gear, not able to shake the feeling that I was being watched.

The private room I was given to work in was a tiny bumped-out porch perfectly suited for tarot card reading. I conducted readings at a cozy table for two warmed by the glow of a cut crystal kerosene lamp. I cherished the space, as it was small and intimate. I appreciated having a quiet, intimate space to give readings as I protect my clients' privacy fiercely.

As a general rule, I advise my clients to wait at least three months between readings. They may want to have them more often, but sooner than three months does not lend itself to manifest change. I do not like to let clients waste their money only to hear the same thing over and over again.

However, throughout a five-year period, I had a client who would visit me every three months like clockwork. She was a very understated person; a bit reminiscent of Toula in the beginning of the movie, *My Big Fat Greek Wedding.* A widow, she lived a very regimented life, never deviating from her daily routines. She would basically eat, sleep, and work, and that was about it.

Yet, when she came to be read, she would always ask me to tell her that something exciting and adventurous was going to happen in her life. As a reader, this can be a difficult situation. It isn't within my principles to just tell her what she wants to hear. I have to be honest and relay what the cards indicate. Unfortunately, because she never veered from her usual routines, the cards always said the same things, as if to convey, "If you keep doing what you're doing, you'll keep getting what you're getting." I often felt as if I was trying to squeeze blood from a stone. Several times I gently suggested that she might want to break out of her comfort zone to stimulate change.

This went on for years. I always felt remorseful when I could not give her a better prognosis, until one day when she requested, as usual, "Tell me an exciting tale!" I spread the cards for her. Much of the meaning was the usual. But then unexpectedly, the Lovers card came up.

I said, "Oh, I see the Lovers Card. You met someone."

"No, I didn't," she replied.

Instantaneously I saw a mini-movie in my mind of her and a suitor in a hot tub, laughing and having great fun. I repeated this to her, but she rejected the very notion. She was adamant that there was no one in her life at all. As a reader, I respected her response and opted to try again. I reshuffled the deck, and sure enough, the Lovers card came up once again. Even though she was vehemently denying it, I couldn't let her objections skew my channeling.

I acknowledged her protests, but with a twinkle in my eye, I advised her, "You might want to keep your legs shaved, because the cards say you're gonna meet a man!"

She pooh-poohed it, and departed.

In spite of my three month-between-readings-guideline, this client returned a mere month later, sweeping into the Gas Light with excitement and exuberance. My immediate impression was that she looked better—brighter somehow.

Without preamble she said, "Oh my god you son of a gun! You were right!"

Nonplussed, I stammered, "What do you mean? What happened?"

She told me that an old boyfriend (now a funeral director) had called her. Subsequently, they rekindled their relationship. He asked her to meet him in Atlantic City. She agreed, and they met up soon after at a popular casino where they had a terrific time gambling, dining, and, believe it or not, they ended up in the hot tub in his penthouse suite.

"As I'm in the hot tub," she said, "I'm thinking, *That son of a gun, Deborah! That girl is good! I can't wait to go back to the Gas Light and tell her that she was so right!*"

∞

The Gas Light restaurant in Ridley Park, PA remains largely unchanged since the late 1920s. Stop in sometime. You may get lucky and meet Gus the friendly ghost!

The Ridley Park Town Clock sits at the center of the Shops of Ridley Park, PA.

Chapter Fifteen

Don't Kill the Messenger

Justice

Fairness; decisions; discovering the
truth; the sword cuts away illusion.

I have had clients who have already decided before we even begin the reading that everything I am going to tell them will be totally wrong. Such skepticism and resistance can shut the channeling down and block the flow, thus creating a self-fulfilling prophecy. Some are so stubborn that they won't acknowledge what I tell them even if it is true.

For example, one night I was giving readings at the Gas Light restaurant. A woman sat down and, unfortunately, I saw nothing positive in her cards. *What should I do?* I thought. I laid the good cards on top of the bad cards to invite Spirit to create a positive outcome.

Card readings are supposed to be positive growth experiences. No one comes to a reading expecting all bad news. For this woman, I was in a quandary as to how to handle this negative information. *How do I find a rose here?* The cards showed that this woman's husband was going to leave her and totally clean her out. They indicated that she would be blindsided and arrive home to an empty house. I knew that she would be devastated to learn this information this way. I asked my spirit guides what to do. They advised me to tell her the truth.

Taking a deep breath, I told her, "Your husband is unhappy. He is worried about your reaction if he tells you, so he won't say what he is feeling. He wants to leave and get a divorce, but he is afraid to tell you."

My client became furious. She started shouting, "How dare you! You don't know what you're talking about!"

I do not take any pleasure in hurting people. Hurting people hurts me. I wish I had thicker skin. She angrily jumped up as if to leave.

Trying to diffuse the situation, I said, "Listen, you don't have to pay for your reading. Obviously, you're upset. I did not mean to upset you, but I get what I get. I'm not wishing it on you. I'm just trying to help you."

She responded angrily, "Well this isn't helping me, and you've got some nerve!"

She threw a little money down on the table and stormed off. This was terribly upsetting to me. I felt awful for the rest of the night. It is agonizing to me to think that I might have hurt anyone. I know that if I lie just to make a client feel better, then I am not a good reader. Good readers don't lie. I was gentle. I didn't tell her the real extent in order to protect her feelings.

Days later I was still upset. Things like this rarely happen. It took a couple of weeks for me to get over it. Less than a month later she returned. I saw her enter the lobby of the restaurant, and I thought, *Oh boy, please don't come in and create a scene.*

The owner ushered her in to the reading room. She had made an appointment, which really surprised me, since she had been so angry last time. I didn't think I'd ever see her again. She sat down at the table, her face soft. I realized that she wasn't there to scream and yell at me.

She said softly and humbly, "I owe you an apology." She continued, "I reacted poorly. I went home and told my husband that I had just gone to a tarot reader, and she told me that you are unhappy and you are going to leave me. I was floored when he confirmed that it was true."

She had asked her husband what was going on. He opened up and told her everything he was feeling. He still ended up leaving, but they split up in a much more amicable way than might have happened. He said that he didn't tell her because he was afraid of her reaction. He confirmed that he had intended to "clean her out" and not tell her ahead of time.

My client was still devastated, but it could have been far worse. She didn't come home one day to an empty, stripped-down house.

"I'm really sorry I blamed you," she said, "but I really didn't believe you. I had no idea he felt that way."

I always pray for the cards to show me things for the client's highest good. Her first reading sure didn't seem like it had been for her highest good to me at the time, but ultimately it turned out to be that way. It was for her highest good for me to warn her. I can sugar coat somewhat, but I never lie. I don't always receive good news in readings, but it usually does end up for the client's highest good.

∞

Chapter Sixteen

Rocco

Judgement

Clearing away emotions from the past; forgiveness not only for others but for the self; emotional understanding; what is heard and answered; new perspective; spiritual awakening.

In the late 1990s, Rocco was a popular teenage athlete at Ridley High. Horrifically, he was hit by a train on New Year's Eve of his sophomore year. When classes resumed after the winter break, administrators announced the tragedy at school. His funeral was held shortly afterwards. The whole situation was horrible. Although I had not known him, I began to experience a deep emptiness, loneliness, and despair. I felt a connection with him, I thought, because I had a son the same age.

My first instinct was to send the family a copy of the book *The Eagle & the Rose*, by Rosemary Altea, which is a wonderful tool to help with grieving. But I make it a practice not to interfere in people's lives unless they seek me out. I endured several days of constant, painful thoughts about this poor boy accompanied by an ache in my stomach. I felt as though he was around me and near me as a restless spirit. Even though his passing to the other side was quick, I got the sense that he hadn't been ready. I felt lingering heaviness and emotional pain. Many would say that this feeling was empathy, as I was the mother of a teenage son myself. That may have been a small part of it, but I intuitively knew this went much, much deeper.

In the following days, everywhere I went I felt his spirit all around me.

A few nights before the visitation I drove over the train tracks. This is a route I travel all the time. Other kids had placed flowers on the tracks. As is common today, it became a shrine. It brought comfort to the kids. I saw so many beautiful flowers, but I had a nagging feeling that there should be candles as well. Amazingly, upon my return trip, candles were there.

At the sight of the teens placing flowers at the shrine, I felt as if a force had pushed me to my breaking point. There was so much pain. I decided I had to try and to do something about it.

I went to a quiet place in my house where I prayed and cried, and asked aloud for the angels to greet him and help him over to the other side. He was trying to tell me that he felt foolish about how he died, and wanted to eliminate any speculation that this may have been a suicide. He communicated clearly that it was *not* a suicide. Now I understood why he had been trying to convey his feelings so strongly.

Suddenly a wave of heightened awareness took over all of my senses. I realized that the Steve Miller Band's song, "Big Old Jet Air Liner," was playing on the radio in the background. I have heard this song many times over, but not in this way. My heightened awareness drew out the lyrics of the song in which the singer bids a reluctant and tearful farewell to friends and family.

This was no coincidence. With chills and tears, it was clear to me that he was relieved that his message had been received. For me a sense of peace and balance had been restored, if only temporarily.

A week or two after my spiritual reunion with Rocco, a new client whom I had never met before, came into the Gas Light to be read. In her cards I saw death, tragedy, and loss. Two cards that immediately stood out were the Ten of Swords and the Two of Pentacles. The Ten of Swords indicated innocence and unexpected forced change. The Two of Pentacles indicated that something was off balance. A familiar sensation of maternal love, warmth, and connection began to build. Spirit had arranged this Divine connection—this was Rocco's mother!

Chills erupted on my left side, as I recognized the familiar signals of mediumship. Compassion and gratitude welled up. I was grateful that she came in to be read because I felt the need to tell her what I had been experiencing regarding her son. She was a very spiritual woman: open-minded, accepting, and loving. The cards turned out to be very relevant to what had happened to her son, right down to the fact that the depiction on the Ten of Swords card resembled him physically. She revealed that Rocco had been celebrating New Year's Eve at a get-together that night, as had been indicated by the Two of Pentacles card.

As the reading continued, another card began to command my attention. It was the Queen of Pentacles. I felt a compelling nudge from his spirit to mention the small rabbit in the corner of this card. When Spirit wants me to relay a specific message, the relevant symbol on the card becomes three-dimensional and is the only thing I can see.

I looked at her and said, "The rabbit is significant. He wants me to talk about the rabbit. What does it mean?"

It turned out that the rabbit was very significant. Her son had made a ceramic rabbit when he was four years old and carried it along on their life journey together. It was a very real and specific message, and a validation of their mother-son bond that went beyond the physical.

At the conclusion of the reading, I could tell that we had gained insight, comfort, and some measure of closure. I hugged her good-bye and wished her well.

Though extremely sad, Rocco's passing seemed to at least have had some positive outcome. It may have served a higher purpose. As a result of this heart-wrenching trauma, many school kids realized the preciousness and fragility of life. Some believe they are invincible. Rocco's story brought the reality home that everyone is vulnerable.

When the news of the writing of my book began to surface, a dear friend arranged for me to meet with Rocco's mother some twenty-one years later. Unbeknownst to me, she had brought her son's ceramic rabbit; the very conduit of our spiritual connection. Tears welled in our eyes as she gently placed the precious rabbit in my hands. I had never before seen it in person. She relayed that after a thorough investigation, which included numerous depositions, the results confirmed that Rocco's death was, indeed, accidental.

My spiritual reunion with this young man was one of the strongest connections that I have ever experienced, proving to me that energy has no boundaries. We really are all connected.

Rocco, thanks for choosing me.

∞

QUEEN of PENTACLES.

Rocco's Ceramic Rabbit

Chapter Seventeen

Ring of Salt

Chariot

Travel; driven by a desire to succeed; balance is necessary to overcome obstacles; determined search for a greater understanding.

A Bucks County client of many years made an appointment for a reading. She was a beautiful young woman who came from humble beginnings, and desperately aspired to wealth and high social status. She ended up marrying a prominent corporate executive, and did indeed achieve these goals.

It turned out that she couldn't handle having so much money, social status, and success. She had acquired too much too fast and succumbed to the eighties zeitgeist of conspicuous consumption and partying. She ended up developing a cocaine addiction. I do not judge people for their life circumstances, but she became a low vibration and devolved into a very draining and difficult client to deal with. She had become a different person from the one she had been when I first began to read her. She was at the point where she needed more intense help, and I had been guiding her in previous readings to find a proper program.

I recently found myself trying to avoid her because she was in denial and not open to change. I felt that a reading would not provide her any benefit in her current state of mind. I knew that my advice in her reading would meet with only resistance and denial. When she called to make this appointment, I felt her negativity and, although I do not like to turn people in need down, my intuition warned me of impending danger. I decided to put a ring of salt around the house for protection from her negative spirit and for prevention of possible bodily harm in light of her irrational state. I spread it most heavily upon the threshold, and asked the Universe that, if it would beneficial to her to have a reading, then allow her to cross the threshold; but if the situation would not be positive, then to somehow prevent her from crossing. This was not a judgement on my part, but caution for my personal safety. I sensed danger.

An hour before her reading, she called to let me know that I-95 had come to a dead stop due to an accident. She said she knew an alternative route and would use it to get to me. She called back half an hour later to tell me that the alternative route was detoured. Another way was blocked. She said, "It seems like it's impossible to get to you today!" Feeling relieved that the Universe had taken this burden off my hands, I told her it was probably for the best as my appointments were now backing up. I told her that she may not have been meant to be read today. Though she was disappointed, she reluctantly agreed and resigned herself to accept that the Universe had other plans for us.

Days later I noticed that my ring of salt had burned the grass, leaving an unbroken, dry brown circle that totally surrounded my house. As if it wasn't strange enough to my neighbors that I was a psychic, now this curious brown ring raised an eyebrow or two.

∞

Chapter Eighteen

I Was Murdered!

Devil

Shadow side; bondage; control; imprisoned;
dishonesty; temptation; lower vibration.

My eyes flew open; my heart thudded in my chest. My breathing came in heavy gasps, and the dampness of sweat clung to my body. Disoriented, it took several seconds for me to realize where I was. The glowing digits on the bedside clock told me that it was two am. I had just awakened from one of the most frightening dreams I have ever had:

> The setting is an outdoor concert—something like a folk festival being held in a state park. I am alone in the dream, which is unusual for me because I would never go to a concert by myself. I am wondering where the bathroom is, as I always do (to which many of my friends can attest.) I can't seem to find one, so I approach a uniformed employee, or someone that seems to work here, because he is dressed like a staff member. He is well groomed with a small beard and has a handsome, friendly face. I ask, "Could you please tell me where the restrooms are?" His answer is long, winding, and very vague. He points in a direction that is away from the concert. My eyes follow to where he is pointing. I am feeling distressed like I will never find it. He asks, "Do you want me to show you?"

> Then the dream flashes to a different moment. I wake up in the passenger side of a car, seat belted in, feeling nauseated and dizzy, like I have been drugged. The car is bumping and jostling. Looking out the window I realize that we are not on a paved road. It is a remote, gravelly, unpaved path. We are traveling

very fast. I look to my left. Driving is the "staff member," who no longer looks friendly. He is dripping with sweat and the grimace on his face is pure evil, like an animal who has just captured its prey.

My dread is palpable. I know now that I am in deep trouble. He is not what he first appeared to be. His friendly mask has fallen away, and his expression gives me the impression that I have become the captive of some evil twin brother. His dark intensity gives me the horrible feeling that he is hell-bent on completing his mission, as he has successfully done many times before. This monster is no amateur. He's got me.

Adrenaline surges through me, battling against the drug induced fog. How do I get out? The lock? The seatbelt? I'm trying not to panic. F**K! I'm passing out again...

I come to again. My clothes feel wet. Wondering why, I look down at my abdomen, where I observe that my once pristine white tee shirt has turned deep crimson. Oh my God, I'm bleeding out! He stabbed me? I feel no pain, just wetness. My life is ebbing, as if the light is going out of me. Now I know I'm dying. At this fateful realization, I resign myself. He has won. He is an animal. I will never forget his face. I remember thinking, He got me. The son of a bitch got me!

I awoke rattled and shaken, not completely sure of what type of dream this was. *Was this remote viewing; was this prophetic, or possibly a past life trauma resurfacing?* In the months that followed, that face etched in my memory, I scoured the news media for any sign of a similar crime, but to no avail. To this day it is still a mystery.

The heavy sensation I experienced from this wildly frightening dream was not so much about the trauma and the fact that I was killed. My intense sense of regret was that I had trusted a pretty face. His normal looks and genial demeanor disguised a deeply hidden evil. We come face to face with people every day, and never really know who they truly are inside and what they are capable of .

∞

Chapter Nineteen

Mom & Dad

The Sun

Marital happiness; harmony; warm climate for pleasure; sharing abundance with others; good fortune shining down; joyful awareness.

My mother was a strong, beautiful woman of the 1950s generation in which one was a lady at all times and kept skeletons in the closet where they belonged. She despised the F-word and believed in the old-school ways of life. Being a good wife and mother was always her top priority. She was ebullient, generous, and so much fun to be around.

She was a young mother during the 1960s and 1970s, the years of Aqua Net and Dippity-Do, hair rollers under scalloped bandanas, and very, *very* big teased hair. Our home was always awash in music. I feel like I had my own personal musical score that defined my childhood and teenage years. When I hear those songs today, (on the oldies stations, of course) each one evokes its own special memory.

I remember times when Mom would have friends over to our modest twin home in the Philly suburb of Collingdale. When all of her guests arrived, she'd announce, "Let's move the table and dance!" Enthusiastically, they would all lift our giant solid oak dining table, set it aside, and then "spin vinyl."

They sang and danced to the sounds of Motown and other hit songs of the time like the Twist, the Mashed Potato, the Bristol Stomp, and her personal favorite, the Jitterbug. Mom made sure the Whiskey Sours flowed as they laughed and boogied down. Her company would later enjoy coffee and the sweet, gooey cinnamon buns that Dad had brought home earlier from the nearby Clifton Heights Bazaar.

During the summers, Mom would invite our cousins and neighborhood kids down the Jersey Shore. There would be as many as ten kids there at a time. Our Somers Point shore house is a modest bungalow set among the Jersey Pines that Great-Grandpop built and passed down through the family. It is simple, but charmingly retro and sentimentally reminiscent of the 1940s era in which it was built. To this day its decor has remained largely unchanged. Most of the furniture, including the ancient table and vinyl-padded chairs still adorn the tiny kitchen as a lovingly battered nod to some of the best days of my life. The pungent aroma of mothballs, camphor flakes, and the musty dampness of the sea air which permeated the bungalow still linger in my memories.

During those days there was no TV, but the bungalow was filled day and night with music from the radio. The only shower was outside at the back of the house. There was always a clamor to be the first to shower before the hot water ran out. The iron-framed beds had old-fashioned metal springs that were topped by thin, blue-striped feather mattresses. Oh, the fun we used to have jumping on those beds!

We'd spend the hot, hazy summer days at the beach. Even though there wasn't much money to spare, Mom made sure everyone had what they needed. She bought bathing suits at the five-and-ten-cent store for every kid. There were no McDonald's Happy Meals, fancy snacks, or restaurant lunches. Mom would buy an entire loaf of bread, spread out the slices, slather peanut butter on one and jelly on another. Then she'd smash them together, and shove them all back into the original bread bag. That was our picnic lunch on the beach. In between splashing in the shallows and jumping the waves, we'd sit on the beach, towels over our heads, sand in our teeth, and munching on our PBJs. It might as well have been caviar. Nothing ever tasted so good!

After a long day at the beach, water logged and sun drenched, we returned to the bungalow. While we showered, Mom would make a giant pot of mac and cheese or spaghetti, and hot dogs in another huge pot. There was always more than enough for everyone, and we often went back for seconds.

Tummies filled, we'd spend the remainder of our nights romping in the yard, catching tiny land frogs and fireflies in a jar, while the adults played badminton. When it got too dark, we'd go inside to play Parcheesi, Pokeno, Monopoly, and Checkers. Then it was up to bed where we'd whisper and giggle until, exhausted from our wonderful sun, sand, and surf-filled day we would fall into a deep and sublimely contented slumber.

Another trait of my mom's that always amazed and awed me, was her knack of knowing when to stand up for something and when to hold back. She was fiercely loyal when someone was in trouble. She would risk her own reputation, and sometimes, even safety to defend the underdog. She wouldn't be quieted just to keep the peace. I remember one time when she fearlessly aided a friend's escape from her abusive husband. The situation had become so dangerous that she sprang into action, rented a truck, drove over to the house and moved the mother, her kids, and their belongings to a safe place.

Mom and Dad were a perfectly matched couple. She was like the sun, radiating warmth and light, and unbridled enthusiasm. Dad was a quieter soul, and was more than content to let her shine. She and my father used to love to slow dance their favorite song, "Till Then" by the Mills Brothers. Even as a child I knew without a doubt that they were true soulmates, as I watched them in each other's arms, twirling around our cozy parlor.

In her early sixties, Mom began to show signs of what would later be diagnosed as Alzheimer's Disease. Over the next decade we watched her slowly slip away to the disease. Interestingly, her instincts about people were the last to leave her. Even in the depths of the disease, she could see through people and know if they were phony or patronizing. If they were authentic, pure, and loving, she sensed it.

When she went to Hospice House, we knew the end was near, and were reluctantly starting to accept it. On one particularly difficult day my sister, Shirley, and I were feeling very emotional and upset at the idea of Mom leaving. The mood in Mom's room was somber and hushed. All of a sudden, we heard a baby laughing in the hallway. It was that contagious, bubbly baby belly laugh. Hearing the baby, my mother's eyes lit up. "Listen to that baby laugh!" she exclaimed, smiling and laughing herself. That was so her. Her joy at hearing the baby's laughter yanked us, for one beautiful moment, out of our unrelenting sadness and mourning. She wanted us to listen to the baby and celebrate the new life.

My father was by her side throughout the excruciating course of this awful disease. He chose to keep her at home safe with him. It was beyond difficult for all of us to watch our beloved matriarch straddle the line between lucidity and dementia. She remained strong in spirit but her continually increasing loss of rational, logical reasoning morphed into a daily hell for my father.

Dad was a hard-working, traditional man of faith who devoted his life to his family. His whole world became the care and protection of my mother, so he lived a largely isolated existence during those years. On their last night together, with a snow storm raging outside, Mom passed away peacefully in his arms at Hospice House, his hand on her heart until its very last beat.

So deeply immersed was my father in my mother's care over the years, that he had paid little attention to himself or the many changes in the outside world. Even though he would always be brokenhearted at the death of his wife of fifty-nine years, he gradually and gingerly began to emerge from the cocoon of caregiving. He knew that he would have to accept that life would now be a "new normal." He had good days and bad, but his natural curiosity and sense of adventure eventually began to draw him out.

We were in awe of everything he had done for Mom, and we wanted to help him to find peace and some measure of happiness. We would now be able to take care of the man who had taken care of our mother with such dedication. We took him shopping for all new clothes. We took him to the eye doctor to remove his cataracts, and to the family doctor to receive all the health check-ups and maintenance that he had put off over the years. He was given a clean bill of health and was on no meds at the age eighty-one. Amazing!

It truly was a new world for him! He couldn't get over it when SIRI gave us directions on my phone. With his cataracts remedied, he was clearly seeing the miraculous beauty of nature and the new world around him. After two decades of limited vision, he literally and figuratively had new eyes.

About a month after my mother passed, she came to me in a dream. I was elated to see her.

Oh, my God, I miss you so much! I told her.

With a serious look on her face, she took my hand in hers and told me not to worry, but that dad was going to have to come with her.

No, please, not yet! I protested, *We need him! It's too much to lose both of you!*

She appeared healthy and beautiful, and was very loving and matter of fact, as if this had already been decided in some big book of destiny. She told me gently that I would be fine, and, poof—she was gone.

I awoke stunned. I knew I had just experienced an authentic reunion dream. I was grateful and happy to have seen Mom again, but very uncertain of what to do with the information she had relayed. *Should I tell the others in the family? How would they react?* I decided to inform the inner circle, but to protect my father, opted not to tell him. Heeding my mother's message, my husband and I made plans to take all of our vacation time and dedicate the summer to my father. We would only do the things that he wanted to do and enjoy every moment of our precious time together.

We headed to the shore house, his very favorite place to be. I alerted family and friends that we would be there and invited them to visit with Dad while he was there. The response was wonderful. We had many visitors at the shore house that summer. Dad enjoyed it immensely. There were dinners with his brother, John, walks on the boardwalk, and soul-inspiring sunsets; some of which Dad cried at for the beauty of it all. He felt a sublime, bittersweet freedom, still aching from the void he felt in his life without his bride.

True to the message of the dream, at the end of the summer Dad had a stroke in my home and passed within days. We were devastated. It had been only eight months since my mother had passed. The poignant words to their favorite song were so spiritually prophetic, depicting separated lovers longing to be together again. Mom mercifully gave us advanced notice so that we could cherish our remaining time with him. They are together now. I suppose they needed to dance in Heaven for eternity.

∞

Alfred Batty, my great-great grandfather built our shore cottage (right) in the 1940s with his own hands.

I love this old photo of my family which includes my grandfather, Richard, Sr.

Dad, Uncle Johnny, Aunt Shirley, and Annie at Cedar Lake, New Jersey.

My bubbly mom and her beloved 1964 1/2 Ford Mustang.

My sister Shirley and I loved our times at the Jersey shore.

Chapter Twenty

Still with Us

Strength

Spiritual strength; a power from love, not force; using compassion to bring harmony; an ability to resolve conflict between the conscious and unconscious.

After my parents passed, my sister, Shirley and I had the complicated task of settling their estate, which included preparing their house for sale. Because of her dementia, Mom had become a packrat. This made going through the house a huge challenge. She had collected, in boxes, all sorts of things: some sentimental and interesting, and others that didn't make sense at all.

We discovered that she had written out cards and letters and stashed them away in unusual places. I would be hard in the moment of cleaning the house out, and just when it would become unbearable, I'd find a card or a letter saying "I'm here if you need me," "I love you," etc. The ironic part was that I always found them when I was missing my parents the most. It was always perfect timing. Some cards contained money. It was as if my mother did not want her daughters to be distressed. All I could think was, *Wow she is still here*. That was the way it seemed.

A lot of the cards involved the word, "magic." Which I found amazing because every time I found a new one, it *felt* magical. I became really bummed when I got to the last hope chest. I knew there would be no more happy treasures to find after I cleaned it out. My birthday was coming soon. To my utter delight there was a birthday card in that last hope chest for me. Its beautiful words were a loving reminder that, though she may not be here in physical form her kisses will find their way to me, and that she is still alive and in the wind.

My father did something similar with two Christmas cards. He wrote a card to my sister and me, but for some reason, never sent them. I found them in a drawer when cleaning out the house. The printing on the cards said "I", which he whited out and changed to "we" to include both Mom and himself as the givers of the cards. Each of the cards mentioned "magic," and that "we are watching over you"—words so amazingly relevant to our situation.

Incredibly, Shirley and I both received a Christmas card from my parents *after* their passing. My parents didn't deliberately stow these cards and letters away to be read after their passing, but that's the way it worked out. I believe it was absolutely Divine.

With heavy hearts, Shirley and I finished preparing our parents' house to be listed for sale. As I was about to close the front door for the last time before the open house, I suddenly felt a tapping on my shoulder. I swung around and there was Mom smiling and waving from her portrait on the wall. Dad had kept it displayed after she passed so he could still see her every day.

Wait! She seemed to say, *Take me home with you! I don't want to stay here anymore!* Then the image of them playing their records and slow dancing flashed through my mind. She wanted to be back with him and with us. Dad's portrait was already at my house where we had brought it after his funeral. It was as if she was telling me, *The Party's over at this house.* I had walked past her portrait hundreds of times since their passing, and this was the first time this had happened.

Now their portraits and ashes are side by side—they are together for all eternity. This seemingly ordinary couple were the most extraordinary people I have ever known.

∞

We wonder if you know
how often we whisper
in our hearts
"God, keep her safe.
We love her so."

Mom and Dad throughout the years.

In loving memory of Richard & Ella May Batty.

Chapter Twenty-One

In the Waiting Room

The Hanged Man

Changing perspective; timing; sacrifice is needed.

After many years of reading cards, I was approached to train to become a hospice emotional support volunteer. It was perfect timing because I had been looking for a way to give back to humanity in gratitude for my many life blessings. As a hospice volunteer, I felt I could use my psychic intuition to mentally understand the wants and needs of a non-verbal patient.

The training was not all that easy, as I was not a member of the medical world. I had had some prior experience with a loved one who passed from cancer, so I was familiar with the stages of crossing over. However, the other trainees were all nurses and familiar with medical terms and procedures. It was a bit intimidating. Nevertheless, I was determined, and after a weekend of training, I was on my way.

As a volunteer, my eyes were opened as to the importance of a life review for the patient, and of trying to completely fulfill the patient's closure bucket list. The patient's desires are first and foremost, and the hospice worker follows the patient's lead at whatever pace the patient dictates. The mind, body, and soul needs of the patient need to be integrated to allow for a peaceful and contented passing for not only the patient, but family and friends as well.

Without being overly graphic, I would like to share some miracles I experienced with my loved ones while in hospice, also known as "the waiting room." Out of respect for the many patients I have worked with, I will only comment on experiences with my own family.

After the initial shock of realizing that one has only limited time in this dimension, a new awareness occurs for everyone involved. We were blessed with a family-oriented hospice that took loving care of us all.

Many amazing things happen during the final stages of death. Our loved ones may "lift off," traveling back and forth between dimensions. Many speak to family members on the other side. Just as in giving birth, the process cannot be rushed. We need to respect the process in spite of how emotionally painful it is to witness.

As for my loved ones, we would play their favorite music and follow their leads as to when to be quiet. Some days we'd pray and cry, and others we'd come in and smile as if it was just another day. I frequently experienced a heightened awareness. Conscious awareness would melt away, and I would simply be in the moment with my family member.

Many nights traveling back and forth to hospice, my sister and I would become very weary, feeling that we just would not be able to go on one more minute, when the *Rocky* theme song would play on the car radio. We took it as a sign, encouraging us to keep fighting and to be strong. It didn't matter where I was, whether in a store getting groceries, at a restaurant, or in the doctor's waiting room. The song would cut through my zombie-like delirium and spur me on.

On one of my father's last days, I was driving home from hospice at five in the morning after keeping vigil for him. I was exhausted, and feeling desolate. While at a stop sign, to my amazement, I spotted, diagonally across from me on the lawn, a giant, eight-point buck. This buck was different than any I had ever seen. He was-so stately and strong. He never moved. He almost looked fake. He simply stood there in the pre-dawn mist just staring at me. It was as if we were both paralyzed. I realized that this buck was strong and majestic, just like my father. I knew this was Dad's totem, and that Dad would "lift off" shortly. He had been a hunter in his younger years, and lived in awe of nature and its beauty.

Death is still a bit taboo for some. Even some patients, as well as their families, just don't want to talk about it. I have learned to respect all views on this topic, without criticism or judgement. For me it has been a privilege to walk my family home with the assistance of a loving hospice.

∞

Taylor Hospice (Residence),

Ridley Park, PA

Chapter Twenty-Two

Final Thoughts

The World

Wholeness; end of a cycle; a completion and success; the journey is the true goal; deeper meaning in life's journey.

I am so grateful for the privilege of having psychic abilities and for being able to provide spiritual guidance to so many over all these years. With every reading and every life experience, I have not only taught, but have been taught so very much. Not all of these truths originated with me, but they are the ones that I believe consistently ring true. I only wish I had been privy to them earlier in my life. It would have saved me a lot of worry and angst.

❖ During mediumship the deceased spirit that the client expects to connect with might not be the one who shows up. I cannot control who comes through because I am simply the conduit.

❖ Reading cards is the great leveler. When I read clients' cards, all facades seem to fall away. Titles, education, money, and prestige just don't seem to matter, as we become simply two human souls connecting in the moment.

❖ One cannot truly understand how something feels until he or she experiences it firsthand. Therefore, I never judge.

❖ A person's consciousness cannot be shifted until they are truly ready.

❖ We never stop growing and learning.

❖ Not everything is a sign.

❖ Nature heals. A way to feel better quickly is to get back to nature.

❖ It is better to teach by example than to criticize. My mother-in-law, Edris, told me this on her deathbed. I never forgot it.

❖ The present moment is all we have. Stop worrying so much about the past and the future.

❖ If it looks like a duck, swims like a duck, and quacks like a duck, then it probably is a duck! Trust your instincts.

❖ As my mom always told me, never be afraid of the dead—it's the living you need to look out for!

❖ Crisis makes you bitter or better. Choose wisely.

∞

AFTERWORD

Thank you for taking this journey with me. I hope that you have enjoyed reading and learning about the life of a psychic, and that some of the information you have learned can help you along your life's journey.

I wish you peace, comfort, and joy,

Deborah Batty Colyer

ABOUT THE AUTHOR

Photo by Gary Colyer, Jr.

Deborah Batty Colyer has been a practicing professional psychic for over thirty-five years. Throughout her fascinating and extraordinary career, she has helped thousands of clients find peace, hope, and answers to their most pressing life questions. Seekers have benefitted greatly from her unique talents in spiritual advising, which include tarot card reading, channeling, mediumship, tea leaf divination, and candle magic.

Made in the USA
Las Vegas, NV
12 March 2024